SENIOR ADULT
Program Builder
No. 2

Resources for fellowship, inspiration, and outreach

Compiled by Paul M. Miller

For the most practical use of this material, it is suggested that the group using the booklet obtain at least three copies: one to be used by the director and the others to be clipped for participants. Please remember that all of this material is protected by the copyright laws and may not be reproduced by any means.

Lillenas Publishing Company
Kansas City, MO 64141

My Shepherd and My Keeper

Help me, Lord, to want to please
Thee;
Help me, Lord, Thy will to know.
Fill my heart with love and praises,
Just because You love me so.

Jesus, Thou art my Lord and Savior;
Jesus rules within my heart.
He's my Shepherd and my Keeper,
He will ne'er from me depart.

Elizabeth Craig Haynes

Recycle Love

The love I have is wonderful;
My friends are good to me.
But I mustn't keep this love;
I must pass it on, you see.

Love is never fully love
Until it finds another
Who can enjoy that love too—
A friend, a stranger, a brother.

So I'll take all the love that's given,
Recycle it each day,
Cherish it and hold it,
Then pass it on its way.

Helen Kitchell Evans

A New Year

Today we begin a New Year,
A chance to walk a new road,
To set our goals a bit higher,
To help carry our brother's load.

A chance to go forward in life,
To show others that we care;
New ways to be loving and helpful,
To be more willing to share.

Today a new world unfolds,
A New Year to try once more;
It is up to us to do better
Than we have the year before.

Helen Kitchell Evans

Sunshine Tomorrow

When evening comes, I like to sort
The happenings of the day
Into heaps of things to remember
And heaps to rake away.

I see no need to try to save
Projects ill winds swept awry.
What's done is done; let's bury the
trash
And let charred embers die,

And use as next day's kindling
Twigs from the happiness heap.
They always burn with a rosy glow
And a joyous leap.

Florence Boutwell

A Senior's Prayer

Grant, dear Lord, this humble
prayer:
Please go easy on my hair.
It's thinning quickly, as You know,
So combing goes painstaking slow
In feeble efforts to disguise it.
Do I succeed? Well, with these eyes,
it's
Hard to tell. Lord, won't You act
To wipe away these cataracts?
And could You ease these aches and
pains,
These 'thritic knees, these var'cose
veins?

On second thought, ignore the above
. . .
Just, please, Lord, fill my days with
love.

Judy Dekker

The Mountain

Once I stood on the top of a mountain,
having finished the climb I'd begun.
It was lovely up there, and no pride can compare
with the pride of a climber who's won.

Life can be like the side of that mountain,
an exhausting and dangerous climb.
There seems no place to rest, on our way to the crest,
and—for spiritual things—little time.

But the view from the top is tremendous—
at the summit, you're nearer the sky.
And, for those who believe, there is much to achieve—
there's a challenge, for all who will try.

I'm determined to conquer that mountain,
though I stumble and fall on the slope.
I've an excellent Guide, climbing there at my side,
and He's holding the end of my rope.

Vernon R. Harris

Christian: Growing Old

Now I have come
From dark years
Into light.
Now I have passed
From ignorance
To spiritual joy.
What can an old man
Write of Christian truth
Except, before a dying hearth,
Enjoy!

The changing weather
Is less noticed now.
Youth
Was the shortest season;
Hours are long.
But moving
With resignation
Into final night,
I sing a wiser,
More contented song.

William Beyer

I Wish

I wish that I could take a peek
In countries far away,
And see what other children do,
And hear the things they say.

Perhaps I couldn't understand
The words they used, but yet
I'd know by looking at each face
If they'd been told, I'll bet.

I'd know if they had heard about
How Jesus loves them, too,
For they'd be smiling all day long
And happy if they knew.

I wish that I could go and tell
The story to each one;
Perhaps someday I'll know for sure
What dimes and prayers have
done.

Phyllis C. Michael

Things Are Looking Up

When my vigor flags and my memory lags,
When I can't hear all you've said,
When the print's too small and the stairs too tall,
It fills my mind with dread.

When I can't sleep nights and I'm scared of heights,
When I doze and nod in my chair,
When the days are long and my heart's not strong,
I'm glad that God's still there.

The sky's still blue, and His Word's still true.
I have food and clothes and air.
The flowers grow, and the pain will go.
The future is bright and fair.

There'll be no more tears and no more fears,
No thought of growing old.
I will see the King, help the angels sing,
And skip down the streets of gold.

Margaret Primrose

The Grumblers

"The Palestine vineyards lay out in the sun;
We'd worked through the day 'til the work was done.
He gave us our pay: we'd agreed on the term—
A penny a day. Yes, we all did affirm.
But look at the others, the ones who came in
At the sixth and ninth hours, some stout, some thin.
Did we not work through intense heat of day?
When they came, the work was well under way!"
Then a voice was heard in the midst of the crowd,
And a deep silence settled down like a shroud.
"Friends, please, listen," He said, "I do thee no wrong.
I've paid what I promised, though the day has been long.
It's lawful to do what I will with My own.
By paying a penny, a lesson I've shown.
If the ones I hired last were given a chance
To come in the morning, they'd have come, perchance.
Though they came late, they've done as I asked.
They've stood by and worked and finished the task.
The kingdom of heaven is here for you all,
Whether you come at the sixth or the ninth hour call."

Eva Staveley

Waiting

I watch from my window day after day,
For someone may come to my door and say,
"I was just passing by on my way to the store.
I really meant to have called before."

"Oh, do come in and sit awhile!"
"Yes," she answers with a friendly smile.
"Perhaps a warm drink and a little chat?
Won't you sit down. I'll take your hat."

I set the tray with special care,
Then tidy my apron and smooth my hair.
"What you've done to this house is such a delight!
And the flowers in your garden are a lovely sight!"

She sips her drink and smiles at me,
As warm and friendly as she can be.
We talk for a while, and then she has to leave;
I feel the urge to tug at her sleeve.

"Perhaps you could stay a wee bit more?"
But smiling, she makes her way to the door.
"Thank you for coming, now do take care."
Then I set the tray down by the empty chair.

I watch from my window and hear myself say,
"Perhaps that will really happen today!"

Theresa V. Meyer

My Quaky Mind

I'm getting so forgetful
  I'm embarrassed . . . it's bizarre!
I can't remember faces,
  Nor where I parked the car.

Phone numbers are contrary,
  And people's names escape me;
I once forgot my home address;
  Some days my mind is quaky.

One thing I *will* remember
  Until the day I die . . .
The name my parents gave me . . .
  It's . . . it's . . . I *think* it's "Sweetie Pie."

Lillian Pittman

Forgive Me, Lord

Forgive me, Lord, for tactless things
  I did and said today.
Allowing busyness to enter in,
  not taking time to pray.

Forgive me, Lord, for grumbling
  instead of offering praise.
Succumbing to my emotions,
  wasting many fruitful days.

Forgive me, Lord, for wandering
  from the path that You had planned.
Now lead me back so I'll rest assured
  of that sweet Promised Land.

Majorie Taylor

Child of God

Dear child of God, be still and know
He walks with you where'er you go.

Dear child of God, you need not fear;
His power to help is always near.

Dear child of God, know all is well,
Since in His love you safely dwell.

Dear child of God, trust Him today;
If dark the path, He lights the way.

Dear child of God, from worry cease;
He is right here now. Rest in peace.

Pearl E. Sisson

She No Longer Lives Here

I think I must warn you,
That if you come to visit her
At the little brown house
She loved so dearly
For 30 years,
She no longer lives here.

Jesus said,
"In my Father's house are many
rooms; . . .
I am going there to prepare a place
for you."
Last week she went to live with her
Father.
But I'm sure she loves her room
In her Father's house
Even more dearly
Than she loved our house.

If you want to visit her,
You must go there.

Geoffrey Stamm

God Gives Me the Language of Love

God gives me the language of love,
The very words I need.

Only love is spoken here,
For Almighty God is living here.
Only His love can give what I lack;
He touches my lips with love.

Only faith is spoken here.
Away with doubts and paralyzing
fear!
My Father gives me the strong desire
to trust;
He touches my heart with faith.

Only laughter is spoken here;
Complaining has no place, that's
clear.
My Jesus gives me grace to see
beyond the clouds;
He touches my world with a smile.

Only words of goodness, never sin,
For the blessed Spirit dwells within.
His mighty power provides all that I
need;
He touches the depths of my being.

Only truth is spoken here;
The enemy has no hold over me.
My Lord gives me wisdom and
insight to clearly see;
He touches my life with reality.

God gives me the language of love,
The very words I need.

Elaine Hardt

I Forget

Memory Lane is a dead-end street;
I'm getting old—you'll have to repeat
  The name you gave me 10 minutes ago.

What is her address? I've looked high and low.
But where did I put it? I'd like to know.
  It just disappeared.

Now as Sally was saying . . . Sally Brown? Sally Green?
She's my very best friend. You know who I mean,
  Do you not?

Well, she had phoned Mary. Or Ann. Or Fay.
Oh, what in the world was I trying to say?
  I've forgotten.

I'm just not as young as I used to be.
I forget a lot. That's plain to see.
  And you see it.

But I know what's important—God's always the same.
He forgave my sins and remembers my name.
  Thank the Lord.

Margaret Primrose

Halfway Home

Retirement—word that seemed so strange to me—
A way of life, all new, 'twas soon to be.
Sometime, yes, but till now just thrust aside;
Around the word my mind had circled wide.
Adjust your thoughts, your life is halfway past;
Its years have come upon me much too fast.
The years you had by time consumed have been;
This time, you'd always thought had been your friend.
But wait! Not end, now bright new phase begins;
There's freedom now, outside of workplace din.
Forget the scars from many battles fought;
Experience has its valued lessons taught.
There is no place to grieve for years now gone.
Look up, and live; you've made it halfway home.

Eleanor W. Cunningham

A Christian Commitment

I will rejoice because of God's mercy and justice,
in a merciless and unjust world.

I will conduct myself in a Christlike manner,
with godly wisdom, in an irrational society.

I will be a Christian role model in the home of my family,
in a world of shattered families.

I will be selective in the kinds of television programs I watch,
in a world of violence and pornography.

I will listen only to music that nourishes my reborn spirit,
in a world of sex- and drug-oriented lyrics.

I will unite in fellowship only with people who do not broadcast gossip,
in a world that thrives on rumors.

I will reinforce meekness and unselfishness,
in a world that is narcissistic, filled with arrogance and vanity.

I will welcome in my home only people who are not deceitful,
in a business world that whitewashes lies.

I will identify only with people who are faithful to Christ,
in a world that proclaims Satan to be God.

I will do these things, Father God,
not with an attitude of holier-than-thou, but with an attitude of love.

I will do these things, Father God,
because I cherish our relationship, even more than life itself.

David Olds

Valentines of Beauty

If I could send a valentine
To everyone from me,
How could I afford it?
What kind would it be?

Would it be all covered
With hearts and frilly lace?
No, my valentine will have to be
A warm and friendly face.

A face that shows appreciation
For the people that I see;
A face of love and inner beauty
Is what it will have to be.

If all would send such valentines,
I think I could guarantee
That peace, not war, would reign,
And all would have true liberty.

Helen Kitchell Evans

God Cares for You

by Orleatha Gravel Kellogg

Scripture: Luke 15:4-7; 19:10

Running time: approximately 25 minutes

Cast:
LEADER—to introduce the program, read the scripture and pray the prayer at the end
HENRY
MILLIE
PIANIST
SOLOIST

Props:
Toy barn with animals—include horse, chicken, cat, cow, pig, sheep.
Sheep—craft—to give as symbol of God's care. See instructions at the end of the devotional.

LEADER *(after reading the scripture):* HENRY and MILLIE are here today to tell us about Dolly, their lost sheep, and the lesson she taught them about God's love for us.

(As the play opens, HENRY *is fussing with the barn and its animals.)*

HENRY: Hey, Millie, come and take a look! I've finished the barn! Just in time too. Tomorrow's little Hank's birthday.

MILLIE: Oh, Henry, it's wonderful. It looks exactly like the one we had on our farm. Hank will be so pleased.

HENRY: How I loved that old barn, Millie! It was the life of the farm, or, I should say, more the shelter for the life of the farm. It protected the animals that gave life to the farm.

MILLIE *(picks up toy horse):* This is a cute little horse, Henry. How fond we were of our team, Barney and Nellie. We never could have run our farm without those horses. Yes, that barn did keep them warm and dry. In that old barn they could rest and be ready for the next day's plowing.

HENRY *(picks up toy pig):* Remember that pen I built in the corner of the barn for the pigs? The sows, with their litters, were safe and comfortable in that barn. I remember that delicious pork you put up in jars, Millie. And how good that bacon smelled in the morning when I came in from doing the barn chores. I was ready for a hearty breakfast by then.

MILLIE: You never lacked for an appetite, Henry. But I don't miss all that work of canning that pork. And what a chore it was to render lard! And, oh, how time-consuming it was to tend the fire when I was smoke-curing the hams and bacon slabs.

HENRY *(picks up a toy chicken):* Do you miss gathering eggs, Millie?

MILLIE: Not really, Henry. Guess I'm lazy in my old age. Gathering eggs was a real chore. Those hens never laid their eggs in the henhouse, where it would have been easy to gather them. They laid eggs all over that barn, in the horse mangers and everywhere in that hayloft. When the kids were home, they gathered the eggs. But even they grumbled. Then as I got older, it became harder for me to climb about that barn, searching for eggs. I never wanted to miss any. We needed each egg to help with expenses as well as for me to use in my cooking.

HENRY: Well, we always had plenty of eggs to take to town to trade for sugar and flour. *(Picks up toy cat)* Look at this cat, Millie. Our barn always had plenty of cats around. They were good mousers too. A barn without a cat begging for a squirt of milk at milking time was not a barn in my thinking.

MILLIE *(picks up toy cow):* We had only four milk cows, but each one was important, as we needed all four to fill those cream cans. That cream, which we took to town and traded for clothing and groceries, saw us through many a sparse year. And we could sell our calves as well as fatten one up to butcher. I'm beginning to really like the thought about that barn being the shelter for the life of the farm, Henry.

HENRY *(picks up sheep):* Here's your sheep, Millie. We kept just a few for your wool. You liked your wool straight from the sheep. And what you couldn't do with it! I remember the quilts you made by using the carded wool for the inner linings. Those were the warmest quilts in the cold bedrooms of our farmhouse. I guess the sheep paid for their keep.

MILLIE: I certainly did enjoy spinning my own yarn, Henry. And I got a lot of pleasure out of knitting warm sweaters, mittens, and socks for my family.

HENRY *(hands sheep to* MILLIE): Remember the day one of your sheep was missing? You were crying, not only because you loved Dolly, but because it was shearing time, and you were planning on making those warm quilts. You had planned to make one for each of our married kids for Christmas, and you needed the wool from all 12 sheep to get the job done.

MILLIE: I'll never forget that day, Henry. But I loved each one of my sheep. I even had given each one a name. That day Dolly came up missing was around the time those wild dogs were roaming the area. I had tried to keep a watchful eye on my sheep, making sure they were all safe in the barn at night. And in the daytime I depended on our old dog, Zeke, to keep an eye on them.

HENRY: Dolly was your problem sheep. She's the one who always found the hole in the fence, and the one who always nibbled her way to trouble. She'd get to eating and wouldn't pay attention to how far she was straying from the flock. Many a time she'd butt and kick at Zeke, who would try to bring her back to the safety of the flock.

MILLIE: But the day Dolly was missing, I forgot all about how naughty she was. I just wanted her back where she belonged. You had to stay at the barn and do the milking. So I set out with Zeke to find Dolly. We searched the ravines and the brush along the fencerows. With Zeke's barking blending in with my yelling, we called and called for Dolly. But there was no answer. And as the sun sank lower and lower in the sky, my heart sank with it. I was sure that some terrible fate had met up with my naughty Dolly. Then when Zeke and I reached the top of the knoll that led us into the western part of the pasture, my heart jumped with joy. There in the plum thicket was Dolly. Her heavy wool was so entangled in the lower branches, it had her trapped. Zeke took off ahead of me, barking his gladness, and I followed as fast as my old legs would carry me. Just as I reached Dolly, I heard gunshots. I was really frightened. Then I turned toward the voice of a man calling to me from the nearby road. It was our neighbor, Ben Monnich. He hollered to tell me not to be afraid, as the shots were coming from the guns of some of the neighbors who were out ridding the area of the wild dogs. He yelled that he had been out rounding up a stray cow and her newborn calf, which he had in tow. He told me he was happy that I'd found Dolly before the wild dogs had. I hollered my thanks and told him I was happy he'd found his cow and calf. And then, even before he disappeared from my view, I knelt right there on the spot and thanked the Lord that those men had been out there working together to rid our countryside of the evil that had been threatening our livestock. Why are you smiling, Henry?

HENRY: I was thinking about that naughty Dolly. She did learn a lesson that day. After that, as I remember, she never fought old Zeke when he disciplined her. She was content to be in the comfort of his guidance. But, Millie, what I was really smiling about is that Dolly wasn't the only one who learned a lesson. If you think about it, we can learn something from Dolly about how much God cares for us. We are all like Dolly. Sheep gone astray. We get tangled up in our sins just as Dolly's heavy wool tangled her up in the plum thicket. She couldn't free herself; she needed you to do that. We can't free ourselves from our sins; we need God to do that through His loving forgiveness.

MILLIE: What a beautiful way to put it, Henry. How comforting it is to know that God's searching love goes after us just as I went to look for Dolly. And the persistence of God's grace searches until He finds us. Why, I wouldn't have thought of giving up the search until I'd found Dolly, dead or alive. How happy I was to find her alive! And how happy God is when He finds a lost soul. And how wonderful it is when we are once again surrounded by God's accepting love.

HENRY: Yes, just the way Dolly felt. She was mighty happy to be back in that barn. The other sheep were happy to see her too. You checked her over to make sure she wasn't hurt. Then she took a good drink of water and settled down in her place in the hay to rest. She was so content that she was safe at last. Just as we are content to be in the comfort of God's love.

MILLIE: Our neighbor was happy that Dolly had been found too. But none were as glad as I was! I felt just as God must feel when a sinner has repented. How happy it makes Him!

HENRY: But there's more here in our lesson, Millie. Zeke helped you with the sheep. In the same way, we are an assistant shepherd helping God. Sometimes God asks us to work alone, in the way Zeke worked alone much of the time to keep the sheep in line. We are to pray for ourselves, and for others, to be strong in times of temptation. And we are to talk to others about the saving grace of God's love. Then at other times God asks us to work in groups. This could be a prayer group or a study group or a committee. It's the way you and Zeke worked together to find Dolly. Or how the neighbors worked together to rid the countryside of the evil of the destructive dogs. That's how God wants us to work together to rid the world of the evil forces against the gospel.

MILLIE: Let's not forget about the barn, Henry. It was a shelter for the animals. God's love, through the Holy Spirit, is the shelter for our lives. It gives us strength, rest, and peace so that we can be ready to do His work.

HENRY: It's comforting to know that we can never wander far from God's love, Millie. He loves each one of us just as we loved each one of our animals. Each animal had a specific purpose on that farm, and each one of us has a specific purpose in God's kingdom. He will not rest until each one of His sheep is home safe in the shelter of His accepting love. It's a wonderful story, Millie. And more so because it's a true story. I think we should write down this story about how Dolly got lost and the lesson she taught us about God's love, so that we can read it to Hank when we give him the barn.

MILLIE: That's a good idea, Henry. Bring me a tablet and pencil, and we'll get started. It's just what we need, a new project now that the barn is finished.

(Song, "The Lord Is My Shepherd")

(Prayer)

Instructions for Making Sheep:

MATERIALS NEEDED: tacky glue, 1½″ and 1″ Styrofoam balls for each sheep you wish to make. Black felt scraps for eyes, ears, nose, and tail. Black chenille wire for legs. Cotton, the kind that is used to stuff toys.

DIRECTIONS: Cut 4 pieces about ¾″ long from chenille wire for legs. Dab a little glue on one end and insert in 1½″ ball. Take one 1″ ball in one hand, and with the thumb of the other, gently shape the face. This will be the head for your sheep. Cut ears, dots for eyes and nose, and glue on face. Dot 1½″ ball with glue and cover with cotton. Glue tail in place.

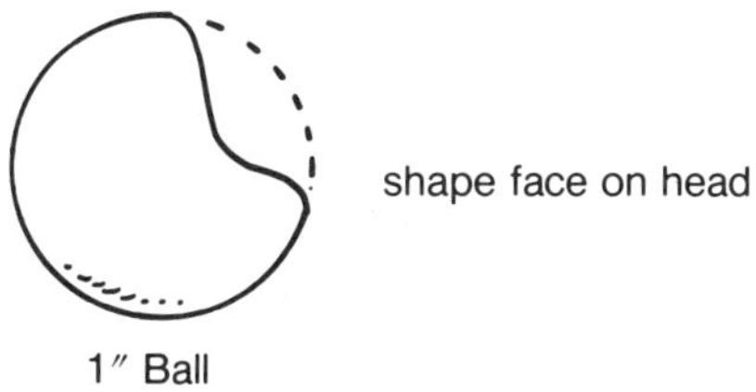

Struck Down

by David S. Lampela

Running time: 5-7 minutes

Cast:
STRUCK DOWN
PERSECUTED

(STRUCK DOWN *enters. Her demeanor is determined but weary. No self-pity. She stares intently at the audience for about 10 seconds before speaking.)*

STRUCK DOWN: I've served my Lord for 45 years . . . faithfully His servant. *(Pause)* Now there's no place for me. I'm old, you see. My children have moved away and . . . my husband is with the Lord. Daily I pray for His leading . . . a word of direction from Him . . . to know my place in His family. He hasn't answered me yet. Or His answer has been to wait. I *have* waited, patiently, but I'm not sure how much longer I have to wait.

No one seems to have a place for me. They don't say it to my face, but I can feel it behind their deference. *(Sarcastically)* "Nice little old lady. Why don't you sit down and take it easy. You've earned the rest." *(Irritated)* What I've earned is the right to *continue* serving my Lord!

I know I'm not what I used to be. I'm old, but not stupid. Bits and pieces of me have fallen away over the years, and the parts left behind have forgotten their assigned function. But there's still plenty of miles left on this ol' girl! If someone would just give me a chance! Sure, a little imagination is needed to find me a spot, but am I not worth it? Haven't I paid my dues?

My eyes are failing, so it's hard for me to teach Sunday School. They say my eyes are too bad to drive anymore, so people are getting tired of running my errands and picking me up for church. My arthritis won't let me help in the kitchen anymore . . . And I lost my choir voice years ago. So what can I do? I still have much to give, but it seems that no one needs me . . .

PERSECUTED: At least you've *had* your chance, lady. At least they still *like* you.

STRUCK DOWN: Who are you? Oh, yes, you're the young man who's been fooling around with the wrong things.

PERSECUTED: Hey, I'm just a free spirit, lady.

STRUCK DOWN: No, you're not a free spirit. You're less free than any of us. You're a prisoner of your own self-pity.

PERSECUTED: You can't talk to *me* like that, lady—

STRUCK DOWN: Oh, yes, I can! And you can quit calling me "lady." I'm old enough to be your grandmother, and I deserve more respect than that.

PERSECUTED: What makes you think you can—

STRUCK DOWN: Almost seventy years of living, that's what.

PERSECUTED: You're no better than the rest. *You* don't like me either.

STRUCK DOWN: You are so busy not liking yourself, how would you know?

PERSECUTED: We're in the same boat. We've both been dumped—just for different reasons. But it works out the same.

STRUCK DOWN: Well, you're right there. *(Sitting)* So, what are we going to do about it?

PERSECUTED: What *can* we do about it? Everybody's against us!

STRUCK DOWN: I know at least one who isn't. Jesus said, "Where two or three have gathered together in My name, there I am in their midst." Why don't we ask Jesus what to do.

PERSECUTED: I . . . I wouldn't know what to say. He won't hear me.

STRUCK DOWN: Let your heart speak for you. The words don't have to be perfect. He'll hear.

(They both bow their heads.)

PERSECUTED *(hesitantly):* Jesus, I know I haven't been the best lately, and You're probably real ashamed of me. But everybody's always yellin' at me and makin' fun of me, and I'm starting to get real lonely. I'd like to have some friends—even just *one. (Pause)* I'm sorry I've been so lousy. Please tell me what to do.

STRUCK DOWN *(after a pause):* Jesus, we claim Your promise. We can feel You here with us . . . and we desperately need Your guidance. We're feeling very much alone these days and need to hear from You. We ask this in Your name. Amen.

PERSECUTED: Well, what do you think?

STRUCK DOWN: Oh, He rarely hits you right in the face with an answer. And sometimes His answer is "wait."

PERSECUTED: Hey, I haven't got all day, lady—er, I mean, ma'am.

STRUCK DOWN: Well, let's see. What can we do while we're waiting? Say, I just happen to have a carton of ice cream in my freezer at home—and I could sure use some help eating it. Besides, with my arthritis, I'm not sure I can even spoon it out.

PERSECUTED: What flavor?

STRUCK DOWN: I do believe it's Rocky Road.

PERSECUTED: That's my favorite!

STRUCK DOWN: The only problem is, I can't drive. I haven't a way home.

PERSECUTED: No problem. I can give you a lift.

STRUCK DOWN: Would you? That would be very nice. If you could just grab my cane for me . . .

(PERSECUTED *bends over to pick up her cane, and a pack of cigarettes falls out of his shirt pocket. He slowly straightens, looking at the cigarettes, embarrassed.)*

STRUCK DOWN *(testing):* You dropped something. You may want those later.

PERSECUTED *(finally turning back to her):* Naw, I won't need them. *(She takes the cane, smiling her approval.)* By the way, when you were praying, the words came real easy. Why is that?

STRUCK DOWN *(chuckling):* Practice makes perfect. I've been talking to Him a long, *long* time. Jesus and I have a real . . . friendship. We get along.

PERSECUTED: *I'd* sure like to know Him that well . . . so that I could talk to Him better. *(Cautiously)* Do you think you could teach me how?

(She studies his face for a moment, checking his sincerity. Then she smiles at him, takes his arm, and they begin walking out.)

STRUCK DOWN: Honey, I could spend the rest of my days telling you about Jesus. *(Pause)* Maybe I can't drive a car or sing in the choir, or serve meals . . . But I can sure tell you about my Jesus.

(Both exit.)

Nightmare of a Shoe Clerk

by Christine E. Scott

Characters:

PERCY PINCHATOE, *the harried shoe clerk*

MERTIE MUSHALONG *and* LUCRETIA LONGFOOT, *young girls quite a while ago*

Setting: PERCY PINCHATOE'S Shoe Store. Three or four chairs in a row for the customers. Several boxes and shoes on display. Cardboard signs announcing sales, specials, as space permits.

(At rise PERCY PINCHATOE *is checking his supply of shoes. He counts, looks around a minute, then goes offstage for more shoes.)*

(Enter MERTIE MUSHALONG *scuffing wearily. She carries an enormous purse and shopping bag stuffed with various articles. There is a large brick in the bottom of the shopping bag. She drops bag with a thump at center, picks it up, grunting.)*

MERTIE: These shopping trips are killing me!
I think I'll rest awhile,
And maybe buy a pair of shoes
If they have a dainty style!

(She picks up one or two on display, drops them, then sinks into chair, groaning. She looks as if at a door.)

I guess the clerk is busy;
I'll just sit here and wait.
Got me some new red flannels,
But suppose they're out-of-date.

(She pulls a pair of long red underwear from her shopping bag. Other purchases could be pulled out and admired. There is a noise at the door, and she stuffs them back into her shopping bag.

(Enter LUCRETIA LONGFOOT, *also carrying huge purse and shopping bag. Hers contains tin pans and spoons. She drops her bag with a clatter at center, picks it up, grunting.)*

LUCRETIA: My big toe hurts me awful!
That means it's going to rain.
I'll just drop down right here a spell
And get my breath again.

(LUCRETIA *limps to chair beside* MERTIE. *They eye each other a moment. There is a pause.)*

LUCRETIA: Your face looks so familiar,
My goodness sakes alive!
Weren't you in Hickstown High School
In the Class of Twenty-five?

MERTIE: Lucretia Longfoot! Gracious me!
How long, dear, has it been
Since we were girls together
Upon the village green?

LUCRETIA: And you are Mertie Mushalong!
Too long we've been apart!
I know I'm going to cry, and there's
A flutter in my heart!

(They scream with delight and throw their arms around each other. They start to cry. MERTIE *pulls extremely large handkerchief from her purse. They each take one end and sob loudly. There is a wet sponge in each end to drip water as they cry.)*

MERTIE: Let's just take off our shoes a spell
And visit if you can!
What have you heard about the girls,
And all our dear old clan?

(They pull off their shoes with difficulty, grunting and groaning. Enter PERCY. *He smiles, bows low, rubs his hands together.)*

LUCRETIA: Young man, we want a pair of shoes!
Our feet are very small!
Sometimes a clerk has such a time
To fit our feet at all!

(LUCRETIA *and* MERTIE *show their feet. They have cotton or crushed paper stuffed inside their hose to give their feet a very long appearance.* PERCY *stares, looks at audience open-mouthed, and measures with his hands with exaggerated gesture.)*

PERCY *(to audience):* I know! They really wear a four!
But now and then a seven.
But then a nine just feels so good,
They buy a size eleven!

(PERCY *goes out after more shoes, shaking his head.* LUCRETIA *and* MERTIE *begin to exchange bits of news. They hold up their hands in astonishment at each item, sigh, cry, scream, etc.)*

MERTIE: I hear that handsome Horace Hatch,
Our star of basketball,
Now plays mouth organ solos
Each night in City Hall!

(They sniffle.)

LUCRETIA: And did you know that Sue Pauline,
The one who was so shy,
Is now an opera singer?
It makes me want to cry!

(They sniffle. MERTIE *again pulls the handkerchief from her purse, and they share it as before, sobbing loudly. Enter* PERCY *with boxes of shoes. He kneels before them, starts trying on shoes. They make terrible faces.)*

MERTIE: No! No! Young man! The style, you know;
It doesn't seem just right.
(To LUCRETIA)
I didn't want that clerk to know
It felt so dreadful tight!

(As scene goes on, PERCY *pulls his hair, groans, tosses the shoes into the air from time to time as they are rejected.)*

LUCRETIA: And you remember good old Sam?
He winked at all the girls!
(LUCRETIA *and* MERTIE *titter.)*
You really wouldn't know him now—
He's cut off all his curls!

(They sob into the handkerchief.)

MERTIE: We used to call him Turtle Head,
He moved so awfully slow. *(Sniffles)*
My goodness, young man, do take care!
You've bent my middle toe!

PERCY: They never will be satisfied.
What is a man to do? *(Slaps forehead)*
With two—young girls—like these to fit
May take a year or two!

(PERCY *tries shoes on* LUCRETIA *again.)*

LUCRETIA: Young man, that pair will never do;
I know they're bound to spread!
(To MERTIE)
That snippy Sally Simpson
Wears a blue wig on her head!

(MERTIE *stares with open mouth. They wipe their eyes, shake their heads, lift their hands in horror.)*

PERCY: Well, never did I see the like!
  Each pair must be just so-so!
Been back and forth so many times,
  I feel just like a yo-yo!

(PERCY *tears hair, tosses shoes, looks desperate.)*

MERTIE: I hear that Josie Jenkins
  Went on a winter cruise!
She buys a twenty-dollar hat
  Each time she gets the blues!

(They both shake their heads.)

PERCY: I had the boxes stacked so neat
  And filed right to the letter!
I think I'll go and drown myself
  As soon as I feel better.

(PERCY *wipes his forehead.)*

(LUCRETIA *and* MERTIE *huddle together, whispering.* PERCY *looks around in desperation, sees some men's big shoes on display. His face lights up. He smirks at audience, taps his forehead knowingly, then picks up the boxes and big shoes with a furtive glance at* LUCRETIA *and* MERTIE. *Then he crawls backward offstage, pulling the boxes and shoes after him, with a villainous grin and a low "Heh, heh, heh.")*

LUCRETIA: And good old Joe—the skinny one—
  Is captain of a tanker!
And mousy little Minnie Brown
  Has wed a wealthy banker!

MERTIE: I met her on the street one day!
  She doesn't have a care!
But I was very shocked to hear
  That she has dyed her hair!

(They are horrified, hold up their hands, sniffle.)

LUCRETIA: She has a row of diamonds
  Around her kitchen sink,
And rubies on the pantry floor,
  And bedsheets trimmed with mink!

(They wipe their eyes.)

(Enter PERCY *with two boxes. He grins fiendishly at audience, gives another low "Heh, heh, heh.")*

PERCY *(very pleasant):* Now here's another model;
I'm very sure they'll please.
You just don't know what comfort is
Until you've tread in these!

(PERCY *again kneels before them so that the audience cannot see what is happening.* LUCRETIA *and* MERTIE *suddenly give big sighs of delight.)*

MERTIE: Young man, these are a perfect fit!
They really are a gem! *(Rises)*

LUCRETIA: They make my feet feel wonderful!
We'll walk right out in them! *(Rises)*

MERTIE: We'll say farewell to bunions sore—
Corn plasters toss away!

(LUCRETIA *and* MERTIE *each pull handfuls of corn plasters and bunion pads from their purses and throw them at the audience.)*

It was so sweet that we should meet,
Dear! What a thrilling day!

LUCRETIA: Let's have a class reunion!
We'll surely make a hit,
We'll dance the light fantastic,
For at last we've shoes that fit!

(LUCRETIA *and* MERTIE *come from behind the piles of shoes and boxes. They shuffle into sight of audience. They are each wearing the shoe boxes and do not realize it. They scuff offstage, tittering and whispering.* PERCY, *still on his knees, looks after them, rises, staggers, and collapses onto his back, legs high in the air for a moment, then dropping them with a loud thump.)*

(Curtain)

Melody in the Heart

by Orleatha Gravel Kellogg

Materials: White poster board—2 pieces (tape together on long side to make a sandwich-type board; in this way it is possible to open to stand as a display board). Paint a large red heart on one side of the poster board. Cut out 5 music notes and a narrow white cross from white cardboard. Glue the notes to the red heart. Cut 5 ovals to fit the body of each note attaching a piece of Velcro to the back of each oval. Print the words LOVE, COMFORT, FAITH, GRACE, VICTORY on the ovals. Place a small piece of Velcro on the red heart just under the dip at the top; color it red. Prepare song sheets of the following hymns for each participant:

1. Blessed Assurance
2. What a Friend We Have in Jesus
3. I Love to Tell the Story
4. Amazing Grace
5. The Old Rugged Cross

People Needed: READER NO. 1, READER NO. 2, SONG LEADER, ACCOMPANIST

READER NO. 1: "Make a joyful noise to the Lord, . . .
Come into his presence with singing!"

This is from Psalm 100. But there are many other places in the Bible where we read that Christians should be "singing and making melody" in their hearts to the Lord. *(Point to notes on heart.)*

The words of a hymn that we sing were first started as an expression of faith in the heart of the person who wrote the song.

Just as music is an expression from a heart, so is our Christianity. The Bible tells us that we do not become a Christian by how many good deeds we do, but by believing in our hearts that Jesus, God's Son, paid God's price to save us when He died on the Cross. In John 3:16 we read, "For God so loved the world that he gave his only Son, that whoever believes in him should not perish but have eternal life." With the heart we believe this and confess with our lips that Jesus is our Salvation.

In the Old Testament we read of many places where music was used to lift people's morale and spirit. One example is David playing the lyre for King Saul; and God used music to encourage King Jehoshaphat and his people to go to battle against a much stronger enemy. He also told

Joshua to blow the trumpets to encourage his soldiers when they marched around the walls of Jericho. As Christians, then, if we truly sing and make melody in our hearts, we can encourage defeated and discouraged friends to trust God and to know that the Savior can give peace and assurance. Music also brings comfort and enjoyment to disheartened people. It has been proven that music helps sick people recover more quickly.

The angels sang at the birth of Jesus. To know Jesus as our Savior is to have all the benefits that music gives and much more. If we know Jesus, He will give us richly all things to enjoy.

We're going to sing about five gifts Jesus gives us.

Number one is LOVE. John 15:9 tells us, "I have loved you even as the Father has loved me. Live within my love." "Blessed Assurance" tells about this trust and love; let's sing it together.

(Place the oval card "LOVE" on a note.)

READER NO. 2: Our hymns give us little sermons on God's Word, what God means to the person who wrote the words to a hymn, and what He can mean and do for us. What a wonderful God we have! He is Father of our Lord Jesus Christ, the Source of every mercy, and the One who so wonderfully comforts and strengthens us in our hardships and trials. And why does He do this? Why does He comfort us? So that when others are troubled, needing our sympathy and encouragement, we can pass on to them this same help and comfort that God has given to us.

The hymn "What a Friend We Have in Jesus" tells us of that comfort. Let's sing it now.

(Place the oval card "COMFORT" on a note.)

READER NO. 1: God has showered down upon us the richness of His grace. For how well He understands us and knows what is best for us at all times. Ephesians 1:4 tells us "we are chosen in the beginning" to belong to Him. Because of what Christ did, all who heard the good news about how to be saved, and who trusted Jesus, now belong to Him.

Let us sing. "I love to tell the story! / 'Twill be my theme in glory / To tell the old, old story / Of Jesus and His love."

(Place the oval card "FAITH" on a note.)

READER NO. 2: "For by grace are ye saved through faith; and that not of yourselves: it is the gift of God: not of works, lest any man should boast." We read that in Ephesians 2:8-9.

The hymn "Amazing Grace" tells how God through the Holy Spirit uses our experiences to convert us from sin to personal acceptance of Christ as our Savior. Let's sing that hymn now.

(Place the oval card "GRACE" on a note.)

READER NO. 1: How we thank God for our victory over sin and death through Jesus Christ and His resurrection! We read of this in 1 Corinthians 15:57-58.

We do not worship the Cross but rather the Christ of the Cross. When we think about the truths of Christ's atonement, we are very much aware of the centrality of the Cross in God's plan of redemption for lost mankind.

We sing about this in that favorite hymn, "The Old Rugged Cross."

(Place the cross in the center of the heart.)

READER NO. 2: Can you hear the melody in your heart? Let's think of melodies in our hearts. "Thank You for the gifts of love, comfort, faith, grace, and victory over death. Help us believe with all our hearts that Jesus Christ is our Lord and Savior, and we will be saved because of His cross. Amen."

What Is a Golden-ager?

by Margaret Primrose

Everyone who lives long enough either gets old or grows old, but nobody thinks of himself as a golden-ager before someone else does.

To some people a golden-ager is one who loses keys, forgets names, takes a dozen pills a day, spills food, uses liniment, hides money under the mattress, stares at four walls, leans on a cane, and sits all day in a rocker. But that doesn't make age golden, and lots of golden-agers paint fences, jog, count calories, use computers, scare people by climbing ladders, piece quilts, travel around the world, and wear out people half their age.

The "older generation" like giant print, low heels, ice cream, cooing babies, short sermons, birthday cards, hugs, and old photo albums. They don't care much for oat bran, contemporary music, motorcycles, short skirts, icy streets, or noise. Most of them remember the Great Depression, the *Saturday Evening Post,* Kate Smith, gored skirts, and lye soap. They like to talk about Fourth of July parades, the Model T, one-toy Christmases, penny postcards, and how hard they had to work as teens. That is not what makes them golden-agers, though.

Golden-agers collect aluminum cans for fund-raisers, buttons from worn-out clothes, snapshots of grandchildren, and paper bags. They may appreciate golf clubs, a handyman, long-stemmed roses, a phone call, or an invitation to dinner, but they hope you won't give them advice unless they ask for it.

Their favorite hymns are "In the Garden," "What a Friend We Have in Jesus," and "The Old Rugged Cross." Fanny Crosby and Charles Wesley wrote their kind of music, and the King James Version of the Bible is their preference.

Time seems longer and shorter to them than when they were younger. They plant flowers, crochet afghans, trim hedges, and ride exercycles, but they are something more than just senior citizens. They visit hospitals, repair toys, dry tears, encourage young Christians, bake cookies for shut-ins, and give generously to spread the gospel. What they have to give may seem little, but it is only the wrapping. Their love is inside the package.

A golden-ager forgets birth dates but knows lots of Bible verses and remembers that you like chocolate cake. He knows when words should be few and also when silence is yellow, not golden. He can be steel or velvet or sandpaper. He says "Thank you" or "Forgive me" with about equal grace.

When one of them promises, "I'll pray for you," you know he will. They're special people to visit when you're hurting. They've hurt, too—not just from arthritis or sprained ankles.

There's a twinkle in a golden-ager's eye when you mention heaven. He may even call it home, especially if life has narrowed him into a wheelchair. A golden-ager knows that before long he will have an address on the golden streets and that age is only golden to those who have that hope. He doesn't know yet if he will sprint or stroll down those streets, but probably both.

Senior Adult Fellowship

by Dorothy M. Brubaker

For a special St. Patrick's fellowship, we consulted our Irish friends and learned that the Gaelic word for a party or gathering is *ceilidhe* (pronounced kay-lee-dee). Also, no *ceilidhe* should be without a large banner with the following greeting: CEAD MILE FAILTE (pronounced ked-mila-fawlcha). Translated, this greeting means "A Hundred Thousand Welcomes."

For invitations illustration see the Shamrock drawing. A poster or banner with the Gaelic greeting is displayed at the registration table. As guests arrive, each is given a name tag and a song sheet (see drawings).

After the potluck, guests participate in a game. Each guest pulls a folded slip of paper from O'Harrigan's Hat. Each slip contains a question. If the guest cannot correctly answer the question, he pulls a folded slip from a second hat. This slip contains a consequence. Both questions and consequences should be in keeping with the Irish theme: such as sing an Irish song or tell an Irish story.

For a devotional, consider a Bible word hunt with the word "green." Check out these references: Genesis 1:30; 9:3; Exodus 10:15; 2 Kings 19:26; Job 39:8; Psalms 23:2; 37:2, 35; 58:9; 92:14; 105:35; Proverbs 11:28; Isaiah 15:6; 37:27; Jeremiah 17:8; Ezekiel 17:24; 20:47; Hosea 14:8; Joel 2:22; Mark 6:39; Luke 23:31; Revelation 8:7.

INVITATION: Exhibit A

CEAD MILE FAILTE
(A Hundred Thousand Welcomes)

Shure an' 'tis tyme
Ta be wearin' o' the green.
Come join our "Ceilidhe."*
'Twill be Irish supreme!

Date: __________ **Time:** __________

Place: ____________________________

Potluck: We'll be lookin'
For some good Irish cookin'.

*Party or gathering.

(Typed on white paper with green ribbon or hand-printed in green ink)

NAME TAG: Exhibit B

Outer shamrock—
green construction paper

Inner section—
white construction paper

Greeting (calligraphy)
in green ink

SONG FOLDER COVER: Exhibit C
(On white paper with green printing)

Céad

Mile

Failte

Sing-along Songs

The Message of the Bells

by Orleatha Gravel Kellogg

Scripture:

Matthew 4:10; Luke 4:16; Psalm 145:1-3; Philippians 3:10

Props:

Bells made in a craft session. See instructions at the end of devotional skit.

Cast:

MARIE

MARTHA

SONG LEADER and ACCOMPANIST

NARRATOR to read Scripture and introduce skit, prayer, etc. May open with song if desired. See list at end of devotional skit.

NARRATOR: Once long ago churches had a high tower where a bell or sometimes two or three bells hung. When the bell was rung, it could be heard for several miles over the quiet countryside. The bell was often used as a communication system for a community. The main purpose, however, was to call the people to worship on Sunday morning. But worshiping God is not reserved for Sunday morning only. We can, and should, worship God every day in our daily lives. Here are two sisters, Marie and Martha, to tell us about the message of the church bells and how they call us to worship at other times than on Sunday morning.

(As the play opens, MARTHA *is sitting quietly watching TV.* MARIE *enters from the side, carrying a set of calico bells.)*

MARIE: I'm back, Martha. Well, I see you're watching TV. Your headache must be better. I'm so glad.

MARTHA: Thank you, dear sister. I do feel much better. Did you have a good time at the craft center?

MARIE: Oh, yes, I did! See the lovely bells I learned to make.

MARTHA: They are pretty. *(She touches them.)* And you did such a good job. The calico looks real country. Where are you going to hang them?

MARIE: I don't know. For now, I just want to sit here and look at them. I don't know when I've made something that has given me such pleasure. I'd like to share a few memories that these bells have given me, Martha. They reminded me of the old bell that hung in that high tower of the small church we attended as children.

MARTHA: I remember our church, and that bell. Its toll could be heard for several miles. It rang out on Sunday morning to call the people to worship service.

MARIE: That bell also rang every evening at six o'clock. Papa said he liked to think the bell was telling people it was time to stop their work for the day and take time to pray, to give thanks to God for the day's labor, and all the other blessings of the day.

MARTHA: Mama always said when the bell rang on a Saturday night that it was to remind the people to get themselves ready for church the next morning.

MARIE: Oh, Martha, that's right. We had to make sure our shoes were polished. We had to lay out our clean dresses and stockings. And we had to recite our Bible verses that were learned for Sunday School.

MARTHA: Mama told us that getting dressed up in our Sunday School clothes was a way of preparing ourselves to go, in reverence, to church, the place provided for the community to worship the Lord. The idea was that the grime and worry of the week were gone, thus uncleanliness was removed. Then, prepared in raiment, in body and soul, we went in to meet the Creator.

MARIE: I remember Mama saying that. It seems just like yesterday. Marie, I am remembering how people would come to church, family by family. Those who lived farther away would come by horse and buggy. Those who lived close by would walk to the church. Usually they arrived well ahead of time for the service to start. And, if the weather was nice, the men would get together to discuss crops and talk about livestock while the women formed another group and discussed their household chores and raising children.

MARTHA: Yes, I remember that. And the children fidgeted because we didn't dare soil our clothing or our hands. But soon the bell would be rung by the preacher to signify that he was ready to begin the worship service.

MARIE: The bell was used for more than calling people to church, Martha. As I remember, it was a communication system for the town. At the time of a death, the church bell tolled once for each year of age of the person who had died. As you counted, you thought about who had been sick, and you could just about guess who had died.

MARTHA: The bell was also our school bell, Marie. It would ring about 8:30 in the morning to remind the children that it was time to head for the one-room schoolhouse. Our school didn't have a bell tower. The only bell was a handbell the teacher rang to call the children in from recess. That bell couldn't be heard much beyond the school yard.

MARIE: The church bell was also used as an alarm system. There were no radios or TVs in those days to alert us of trouble. The bell rang and rang in a way you knew it was something urgent. It wasn't the rhythmical tolling of the other events, and since it would be at an odd time of the day, folks knew there was trouble of some sort. It might have been a fire, a storm warning, or a lost child or an animal, or any disaster. People dropped what they were doing and assembled at the church to find out what the trouble was and how they could help.

MARTHA: That church bell truly served the community. All this remembering has got me missing the worship service in that little country church. I miss going to church, period. Here I am stuck in this house! A shut-in! I feel so cut off from the church.

MARIE: I suppose you do, Martha. But the church is not a building. The church is in the hearts of Christians. And we can worship God in other ways when we can't get to the house provided for worship.

MARTHA: I know that, Marie. I learned that way back as a child in Sunday School!

MARIE: The pastors call on you, the deacons come to give you Communion, and the women from Lydia Circle come to visit you. I'd say you are hardly forgotten, Martha. And another thing—you listen to our church service on the radio every Sunday. And I always bring the church bulletin home for you to read along with many greetings from your Christian friends.

MARTHA: I do appreciate all you and the church folks do, Marie. I do get a lot of comfort listening to the service over the radio. And I do feel a part of it because I try to participate by singing along on the hymns, repeating the prayers, and so on. I guess the radio is a bell calling me to church.

MARIE: Yes, it could be that, Martha. Remember Pastor Hansen saying last Sunday that worship is a time set aside so that a person can think about God and His purposes. He pointed out that adoration of and devotion to God involves adoration of His loving purpose and righteous will. To do that we have to commune with Him. To really get to know Him takes more than sitting one hour a week on a church pew. Just as that church bell rang every evening, Martha, so should worship of God be daily. There are lots of ways we can worship Him. Reading the Bible is one. Whether we read it together or alone, we are getting to know Him. And that is worship, Martha.

MARTHA: Well, then, if you put it that way, I'd have to add that prayer is another way of worshiping God. Praising Him for His kindnesses and mercies and thanking Him for the countless blessings we enjoy every day is certainly adoration of His loving purpose and righteous will that Pastor Hansen was telling us about. Prayer is communing with God. Prayer tells Him we have a desire to have fellowship with Him. Through prayer we can talk to Him about our failures, about our wrong decisions, about our indifference to the welfare of others, and all other wrongdoing. Oh, my, praying is more than a table grace, that's for sure. We must not forget that we talk to God not only about our own hurts but also about those of other people we love. Marie, it is wonderful to talk with Him anytime of the day!

MARIE: It's like the song "What a Friend We Have in Jesus." Yes, Martha, I agree with you, praying is worshiping God. There's another message of the bells that tells us a way of worshiping Him. The church bell rang in the mornings to call us to our schoolhouse. Worship is God's schoolhouse in a way. We learn about Him from the teachings of Jesus. His teachings reveal God's love, goodness, and majesty.

MARTHA: Well, Jesus taught that we should love one another. That could be the message of the bell that rang so urgently whenever there was a disaster. I believe that all my Christian friends who come to call on me, or to call on those in the hospitals, are answering the bell of help needed. This also includes the ladies of the church who serve funeral lunches or collect clothing and food for the needy. Serving others in the name of Jesus is indeed a way of worshiping God.

MARIE: Well, these bells really told us a lot about worshiping God, Martha. I believe that I'll hang them right here on the wall behind the TV. That way every time we look at them, we will be reminded of their message to worship God at all times in all ways as we go about our daily tasks.

MARTHA and MARIE: Praise be to God!

(Prayer)

MUSIC: Suggested list—select number for time allotted

Oh, Worship the King
Praise Ye the Lord, the Almighty
Now Thank We All Our God
What a Friend We Have in Jesus
How Great Thou Art

BELL ORNAMENT: Can make a string of two or three as desired.

Finished size is approximately 5″. Use bright scraps of calico. Cut two from pattern. Pin right sides together. Insert a small loop of rickrack, yarn, ribbon, or thread at the dot with the loop inside, between layers, raw edges matching. Sew from notch to notch, leaving opening between the notches. Trim corners carefully. Turn. Stuff bell softly. Turn in bottom edges. Close with a hand stitch. Attach jingle bell at center bottom.

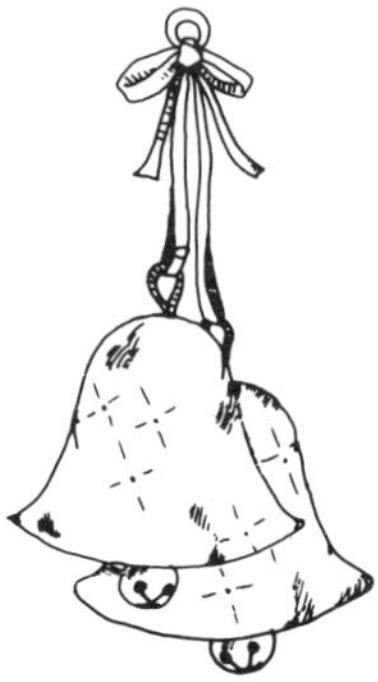

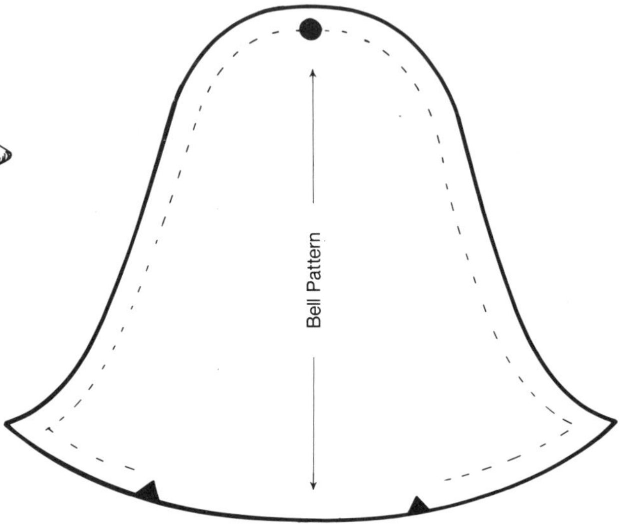

To hang on wall or door, use matching or contrasting yarn or ribbon to make a bow. Take another length of ribbon or yarn and thread through loops on bell tops and attach to bow. Sew a small ring on bow for hanging on wall or door.